Book Of Jokes

I've always thought that laughing is one of the best things in life. Whether it's a funny joke, a classic dad joke, or a silly one-liner that makes you roll your eyes—I love them all. That's why I put this book together.

Inside, you'll find a bunch of jokes that made me laugh, chuckle, or shake my head. Some are old favourites, some are super cheesy, and others are the kind of jokes you'll want to share (or groan at).

But this book isn't just jokes. I've also added a part about the history of jesters—the funny people who made kings and queens laugh a long time ago. They remind us that laughter has always been important, no matter where you are.

This book is for anyone who loves a good laugh, a bad joke, or just wants to feel happier. Open it to any page, and you'll find something to make you smile. The cheesier the joke, the funnier it is!
Enjoy the laughs—and don't forget to share them!

Knock knock jokes

Knock, knock.
Who's there?
Woo.
Woo who?
Glad you're excited, too!

Knock, knock.
Who's there?
Lettuce.
Lettuce who?
Lettuce in, it's cold out here!

Knock, knock.
Who's there?
Etch.
Etch who?
Bless you!

Knock, knock.
Who's there?
Boo.
Boo who?
Don't cry, it's just a joke.

Knock, knock.
Who's there?
Anita.
Anita who?
Anita use your bathroom.

Knock, knock.
Who's there?
Dozen.
Dozen who?
Dozen anyone want to let me in?

Knock, knock.
Who's there?
Wafer.
Wafer who?
Wafer me, I'm coming!

Knock, knock.
Who's there?
I need up.
I need up who?
Can you hold it in? I'm in the middle of a joke.

Knock, knock.
Who's there?
I eat mop.
I eat mop who?
Gross!

Knock, knock.
Who's there?
Closure.
Closure who?
Closure mouth!

Knock, knock.
Who's there?
Avenue.
Avenue who?
Avenue heard this joke before?

Knock, knock.
Who's there?
Doris.
Doris who?
Doris locked, that's why I'm knocking!

Elizabeth Ryam

Knock, knock.
Who's there?
Honeycomb.
Honeycomb who?
Honeycomb your hair, it's a mess!

Knock, knock.
Who's there?
Wendy.
Wendy who?
Wendy you think we can go on a date?

Knock, knock.
Who's there?
Spell.
Spell who?
W-h-o.

Knock, knock.
Who's there?
Repeat.
Repeat who?
Okay... who, who, who!

Knock, knock.
Who's there?
Ice cream.
Ice cream who?
Ice cream if you don't give me some candy.

Knock, knock.
Who's there?
Wire.
Wire who?
Wire you so cute?

Knock, knock.
Who's there?
Owls.
Owls who?
Yes, they do!

Knock, knock.
Who's there?
Auto.
Auto who?
You auto know it's me by now.

Knock, knock.
Who's there?
Sherwood.
Sherwood who?
Sherwood like to be your friend!

Knock, knock.
Who's there?
Doorbell repairman.

Knock, knock.
Who's there?
Yukon.
Yukon who?
Yukon tell me the next joke, I'm tired.

Knock, knock.
Who's there?
Toucan.
Toucan who?
Toucan play this game!

Knock! Knock.
Who's there?
Peas.
Peas who?
Peas open the door for me!

Knock! Knock.
Who's there?
Iva.
Iva who?
Iva sore hand from knocking!

Knock! Knock.
Who's there?
Isadore.
Isadore who?
Isadore made out of wood?

Knock! Knock.
Who's there?
Norma Lee.
Norma Lee who?
Norma Lee I'd use the doorbell, but it's broken.

Knock! Knock.
Who's there?
Needle.
Needle who?
Needle little help here...the door is stuck.

Knock! Knock.
Who's there?
Ben.
Ben who?
Ben knocking for 10 minutes!

Knock! Knock.
Who's there?
Moustache.
Moustache who?
I moustache you a question, but I'll shave it for later.

Knock! Knock.
Who's there?
Candice.
Candice who?
Candice joke get any worse?

Knock, knock.
Who's there?
Noah.
Noah who?
Noah good joke to tell?

Knock, knock.
Who's there?
Annie.
Annie who?
Annie body home?

Knock knock.
Who's there?
Cereal.
Cereal who?
Cereal-ously, open the door!

Knock, knock.
Who's there?
Amos.
Amos who?
A mosquito bit me!

Knock, knock.
Who's there?
Andy.
Andy who?
And he bit me again!

Knock, knock.
Who's there?
Snow.
Snow who?
Snow use—these jokes will never be funny.

Bar jokes

The past, present, and future walk into a bar.
It was tense.

A guy walks into a bar with a piece of asphalt under his arm.
He asks for one beer, and one for the road.

A neutron walks into a bar.
"How much for a beer?" the neutron asks.
"For you?" says the bartender. "No charge."

A five-dollar bill walks into a bar.
The bartender says, "Hey. This is a singles bar.

Two guys walk into a bar.
The third one ducks.

A weasel walks into a bar.
The bartender says, "Wow, I've never served a weasel before. What can I get you?"
"Pop," goes the weasel.

A sandwich walks into a bar.
The bartender says, "Sorry, sir. We don't serve food here."

A tennis ball walks into a bar.
The barman says, "Have you been served?"

Two jumper cables walk into a bar.
One of them says, "We'd like a couple of beers, please."
The bartender says, "OK, but don't start anything."

A new lawyer walks into a diner.
"Where's the bar?" she asks.
A waiter responds, "You passed it on the way here."

A goldfish walks into a bar and looks at the bartender.
The bartender asks, "What can I get you?"
The goldfish says, "Water."

A duck walks into a bar,
orders a drink, and says to the bartender,
"Put it on my bill."

A mushroom walks into a bar.
The bartender says, "I'm sorry, we don't serve your kind in here."
The mushrooms replies, "Why not? I'm a fungi!"

A calculus teacher walks into a bar, and orders a Coke.
The bartender says, "Can't I get you something stronger?"
The calculus teacher says, "Sorry, but I can't drink and derive."

Charles Dickens walks into a bar and orders a martini.
The bartender asks, "Olive or twist?"

A guy walks into a bar, sits down and hears a small voice say, "You look nice today."
A few minutes later he again hears a small voice say, "That's a nice shirt."
The guy asks the bartender, "Who is that?"
The bartender says, "Those are the peanuts. They're complimentary!"

A dyslexic guy walks into a bra.

An amnesiac walks into a bar and asks the bartender,
"Do I come here often?"

A ghost walks into a bar.
The bartender says, "Sorry, we don't serve spirits here."

A Roman walks into a bar, holds up two fingers, and says,
"I'll have five beers, please."

A limbo champion walked into a bar.
He was immediately disqualified.

Gold walks into a bar.
The bartender yells, "AU, get out!"

An unruly football rolls into a bar.
The bartender kicked him out.

A bra, a battery and a set of jump leads go into a bar.
The bra orders 3 pints of larger.
The barman says "Sorry, I'm not serving you. You're off your t*ts and the other two look like they might start something".

A dung beetle walks into a bar and asks, "Is this stool taken?"
A man with authority walks into a bar.
He orders everyone around.

I walked into a bar last night, got a terrible headache.
It was an iron bar…

An Irishman walks by a bar… it could happen.

David Hasselhoff walks into a bar and says to the barman,
"I want you to call me David Hoff."
The barman replies "sure thing, Dave… no hassle."

A guy walks into a bar and asks for fruit punch the bartender says "sure just get in line".
The guy looks over and gets confused cause there's no punchline.

A perfectionist walked into a bar.
Apparently, the bar wasn't set high enough.

Who do ghosts like to haunt bars?
Free boos.

 So Jesus walks into a bar and says,
"I'll just have a glass of water."

History of Jesters

Jesters have a rich history, often acting as entertainers, observers, and critics in royal courts and various social settings.

Early Beginnings

The tradition of jesters goes back to ancient civilisations, though they were not always called "jesters" in those times. In Ancient Egypt, for example, the Pharaohs employed entertainers who performed comedic skits and playful mockery for the royal court, often including comedic skits and playful mockery. Similarly, the Greeks had "fools" or "comic actors" in their plays who would perform for the elite.

The word "jester" in English wasn't used until the mid-16th century, during Tudor times. It comes from the older French word "gestour" (meaning storyteller or minstrel). Before "jester," there were other terms like "buffoon," and "bourder."

Medieval Times

In the Middle Ages, the role of the jester really took shape. Often called "fools," these entertainers were tasked with bringing humour and joy to the otherwise serious lives of the nobility. Their colourful costumes and witty remarks were central to their identity, and their performances helped to lighten the often serious and tense atmosphere. They were usually the only ones allowed to mock or criticise the king and his court without fear of punishment, which gave them a unique form of influence. Skilled in satire and humour, they used their position to address sensitive or controversial topics, entertaining the powerful, and reflecting societal truths. they revealed truths and made sharp remarks that were often overlooked or excused due to their role.

The Jester's Performances

Jesters would perform all kinds of acts to entertain—comedy, juggling, acrobatics, singing, and storytelling. They wore distinctive costumes—often colourful and flamboyant, with hats decorated with bells or "ears," marking them as distinct from the rest of the court. The classic "fool's cap," with its three points, was thought to represent the three traits of a fool: ignorance, madness, and folly. These colourful outfits not only entertained but also highlighted their role as outsiders, keeping things light-hearted while poking fun at the serious world around them.

The Fool and the King

Jesters had a pretty unique and contradictory role in the court. While they were often seen as lower ranking, they enjoyed a freedom that others didn't have. Their humour could poke fun at the powerful, challenge authority, and even offer a kind of "court wisdom." In some cases, jesters became so influential that they gained the trust of kings and queens, even becoming their close advisors or confidants.

Notable Jesters

· **Richard II's Jester:** One of the most famous jesters in history, Richard II's jester, known as "Touchstone," had a pretty unique role in court. Known for his sharp humour and clever wordplay, he often acted as the voice of reason in a place that took itself way too seriously.

· **Tarlton:** Will Kempe, a well-known Elizabethan actor and jester, was another big name. He was a contemporary of Shakespeare and even performed in many of the Bard's plays.

· **King Lear's Fool:** The Fool in King Lear is one of the most iconic literary jesters. He wasn't just comic relief—his wit and riddles helped him challenge the king, speaking truths that others couldn't.

Decline of the Jester

By the 17th century, the jester's role began to fade with the rise of professional theatre, where comedic actors took over many of the jester's functions. The decline of monarchy and the changing social dynamics also contributed to the reduced need for a dedicated court fool. However, the archetype of the "fool" persists in literature, theatre, and modern-day performance arts. The character lives on in comedy and shows today, often serving as the one who speaks uncomfortable truths and hides wisdom in humour.

Dark Humour

I told my wife she was drawing her eyebrows too high.
She looked surprised.

Why don't graveyards ever get overcrowded?
Because people are dying to get in.

My boss told me to have a good day...
So I went home.

What's the difference between a well-dressed man on a unicycle and a poorly dressed man on a bike?
Attire.

I have a joke about time travel,
but you didn't like it.

Parallel lines have so much in common.
It's a shame they'll never meet.

Why don't skeletons fight each other?
They don't have the guts.

Claustrophobic people are more productive...
because they think outside the box.

I'd tell you a construction joke,
but I'm still working on it.

I used to play piano by ear,
but now I use my hands.

I have a stepladder because my real ladder left when I was a kid.

The man who invented autocorrect should burn in hello.

My therapist says I have a preoccupation with vengeance.
We'll see about that.

I'm great at multitasking.
I can waste time, be unproductive, and procrastinate all at once.

Elizabeth Ryam

I told my friend 10 jokes to make him laugh.
Sadly, no pun in ten did.

Why don't orphans play hide-and-seek?
Because good luck hiding when no one's looking for you.

My memory has gotten so bad it's caused me to lose my job.
I'm still employed—I just can't remember where.

I threw a boomerang a few years ago.
I now live in constant fear.

People say nothing is impossible,
but I do nothing every day.

I broke my arm in two places.
My doctor told me to stop going to those places.

I named my dog 'Five Miles' so I can say I walk Five Miles every day.

I told my friend I was cold,
so he told me to go stand in the corner. It's 90 degrees.

Why don't skeletons go to parties?
They have no body to go with.

I used to be indecisive,
but now I'm not sure.

I asked my dog what's two minus two.
He said nothing.

I have a fear of speed bumps,
but I'm slowly getting over it.

What's red and bad for your teeth?
A brick.

I used to hate facial hair,
but then it grew on me.

Why did the scarecrow win an award?
He was outstanding in his field.

I'd tell you a joke about paper,
but it's tearable.

I have a joke about broken pencils,
but it's pointless.

I used to be a banker,
but I lost interest.

I wasn't originally going to get a brain transplant,
but I changed my mind.

Why did the picture go to jail?
Because it was framed.

What's worse than finding a worm in your apple?
Finding half a worm.

Anecdotal jokes

I once signed up for a marathon thinking it would be fun.
They said it was a 'run for charity,' but after mile two, I realised the only thing I was running from **was my poor life choices.**

I decided to take up gardening to relax
Planted some flowers, watered them daily, and even talked to them. After a week, they still died. **Turns out plants aren't into small talk.**

I once tried to impress someone by cooking dinner from scratch.
I burned the chicken, overcooked the pasta, and somehow set off the smoke alarm. The only **thing I successfully made was a phone call to the local pizza place.**

I tried learning a new language with an app.
After two weeks, I proudly greeted my neighbour in Spanish. She stared at me, shook her head, **and replied, 'I speak English.**

I once tried to catch fog.
Mist.

I once bought a belt made entirely of watches.
It was a complete waist of time."

I told my friend I'd make a joke about chemistry,
but I didn't think I'd get a reaction.

I accidentally swallowed some food colouring once.
The doctor said I'm fine, but I feel like I've dyed a little inside.

I once had a job as a human cannonball at a circus.
But I got fired. Guess they found someone of higher caliber.

I opened a bakery once,
but I couldn't make enough dough.

I tried to start a hot air balloon business.
It never really took off.

I once tried to play hide-and-seek in the hospital.
Turns out good health is really hard to find.

I decided to start meditating to clear my mind.
Five minutes in, I achieved total peace—right after overthinking my entire life, planning dinner, **and remembering that embarrassing thing I did in 2012**

I thought adulthood would come with wisdom.
It did. I'm now wise enough to realise I have no idea what I'm doing.

A boy walks into a barbershop. The barber whispers to his customer, "That kid's the dumbest. Watch this."
He holds out a five-dollar bill in one hand and two one-dollar coins in the other. "Which do you **want, kid?"**
The boy grabs the coins and leaves.
"See? Never learns," the barber laughs.
Later, the customer sees the boy eating ice cream and asks,
"Hey, why'd you take the coins instead of the five?"
The boy grins, "Because the day I take the five, the game's over."

Pessimist: Oh, this can't get any worse!
Optimist: Yes, it can!

A man finds a parking ticket on his car.
He sighs, pulls out his wallet, and mutters,
"Well, at least now I've paid for parking."

A guy walks into a library and asks, "Can I get a burger and fries?"
The librarian whispers, "Sir, this is a library."
He nods, then whispers back, "Oh, sorry... can I get a burger and fries?"

I set my alarm for 6 AM to be productive.
When it went off, I thought, "Wow, that was a good idea."
Then I went back to sleep, proud of my planning.

I asked the café owner, "What's the Wi-Fi password?"
He said, "You need to buy a coffee first."
So I bought one and asked again.
He replied, "You need to buy a coffee first—all lowercase, no spaces."

During a logic exam, the question was: "Explain the difference between ignorance and apathy."
A student wrote: "I don't know, and I don't care."
They got full marks.

Cheesy, Dad Jokes

I only know 25 letters of the alphabet. I don't know y.

I told my wife she was drawing her eyebrows too high. She looked surprised.

I used to play piano by ear, but now I use my hands.

What do you call fake spaghetti? An impasta.

I would tell you a joke about construction, but I'm still working on it.

What's brown and sticky? A stick.

Did you hear about the kidnapping at school? It's fine—he woke up.

I bought some shoes from a drug dealer. I don't know what he laced them with, but I was tripping all day.

Why don't eggs tell jokes? They'd crack each other up.

I'd tell you a joke about time travel, but you didn't like it.

Why did the golfer bring two pairs of pants? In case he got a hole in one.

Why did the math book look sad? It had too many problems.

How does a penguin build its house? Igloos it together.

I used to be addicted to soap, but I'm clean now.

Why don't skeletons fight each other? They don't have the guts.

Did you hear about the restaurant on the moon? Great food, no atmosphere.

I would avoid the sushi if I were you. It's a little fishy.

What do you call an alligator in a vest? An investigator.

Why can't you give Elsa a balloon? Because she'll let it go.

How does the ocean say hi? It waves.

Why did the coffee file a police report? It got mugged.

I told my wife she should do lunges to stay in shape. That was a big step forward.

How do you organise a space party? You planet.

Why did the tomato turn red? Because it saw the salad dressing.

I'm reading a book about anti-gravity. It's impossible to put down.

What do you call a snowman with a six-pack? An abdominal snowman.

Why can't bicycles stand on their own? They're two-tired.

I got hit in the head with a can of soda. Luckily, it was a soft drink.

Why don't crabs give to charity? Because they're shellfish.

I told my computer I needed a break, and now it won't stop sending me Kit-Kats.

What did the big flower say to the little flower? Hi, bud!

I used to be afraid of hurdles, but I got over it.

I'm on a seafood diet. I see food, and I eat it.

How do you make holy water? You boil the hell out of it.

Why did the stadium get hot after the game? All the fans left.

What do you call a can opener that doesn't work? A can't opener.

Why did the man get hit by a bike every day? He was stuck in a vicious cycle.

What do you call a snowman's dog? A slush puppy.

I couldn't figure out how to put my seatbelt on. Then it just clicked.

Why can't you hear a pterodactyl go to the bathroom? Because the "P" is silent.

What do you call a bear with no teeth? A gummy bear.

How do you find Will Smith in the snow? Look for fresh prints.

Why was the math teacher suspicious of prime numbers? They were acting odd.

Why did the grape stop in the middle of the road? It ran out of juice.

What do you call a magician who's bad at magic? Ian.

How do you catch a squirrel? Climb a tree and act like a nut.

What do you call two birds in love? Tweethearts.

Why are elevator jokes so good? They work on many levels.

What's a ninja's favourite type of shoes? Sneakers.

What do you call a cow with no legs? Ground beef.

Why don't ants ever get sick? Because they have tiny ant-bodies.

How does the moon cut its hair? Eclipse it.

I'm reading a book on the history of glue. I just can't seem to put it down.

What do you call a dog that can do magic? A Labracadabrador.

Did you hear about the claustrophobic astronaut? He needed a little space.

Why do bees have sticky hair? Because they use honeycombs.

I asked the librarian if the library had books on paranoia. She whispered, "They're right behind you."

When does a joke become a dad joke? When the punchline becomes apparent.

Did you hear the one about the guy who ate a frog? He's probably going to croak.

What do you call a cold puppy? A chilli dog.

I put my old car in reverse and thought,
"Wow, this really takes me back."

I told my mum I'd call her later, but she said she prefers "Mum."

Why did the spider go to school? He wanted to be a web designer.

What do you call a fly without wings? A walk.

Two fish are in a tank. One turns to the other and says, "Any idea how to drive this thing?"

I don't tell dad jokes that often. But when I do, he laughs.

What did the pirate say on his birthday? "Aye, matey!"

I'd tell you a joke to end this book... but I'm afraid it might be the last straw.

Printed in Great Britain
by Amazon

59751155R00020